INDEPENDENT AND UNOFFICIAL

THE ESSENTIAL
HANDBOOK
FOR NINTENDO SWITCH

MORTIMER

Published in 2022 by Mortimer Children's
An Imprint of Welbeck Children's Limited,
part of Welbeck Publishing Group.
Based in London and Sydney.
www.welbeckpublishing.com

ISBN 978 1 83935 170 9

Printed in Dongguan, China

10 9 8 7 6 5 4 3 2 1

Text and Design: Dynamo Limited
Design Manager: Sam James
Editorial Manager: Joff Brown
Production: Melanie Robertson

INDEPENDENT AND UNOFFICIAL

THE ESSENTIAL

HANDBOOK

FOR NINTENDO SWITCH

Contents

6   **Introduction**
Secrets of the Switch
8   **Take the case**
10 **Story of the Switch**
12 **Gamer's guide**
14 **Quiz: Game selector**

16 **It's-a Mario!**
Intro and Super Mario Odyssey
18 **Mario Golf Super Rush, Super Mario 3D All-Stars**
20 **Mario Kart 8 Deluxe**
22 **Super Mario Party, Mario Party Superstars,**
Super Mario Maker 2,Super Mario 3D World +
Bowser's Fury
24 **Mario Tennis Aces,**
Mario and Sonic at the Olympic Games,
Paper Mario: The Origami King
26 **Luigi's Mansion 3, Retro Mario**
28 **Quiz: Your ideal Mario**

30 **Small but beautiful**
Untitled Goose Game
32 **Cuphead, Among Us, Night in the Woods**
34 **The Escapists, Donut County, Sayonara Wild Hearts**

36 **Pokémon games**
Intro and Pokémon Sword and Shield
38 **Pokémon Let's Go Pikachu/Eevee. Pokémon**
Legends: Arceus, Pokémon Unite, Pokémon Snap
40 **Quiz: Pokémon game selector**

42 **Get-up-and-go games**
Ring Fit Adventure
44 Just Dance, Fitness Boxing, Arms, Carnival Games

46 **Cross-platform classics**
Minecraft, Minecraft Dungeons,
FIFA, Rocket League
48 Fortnite, Hades, Monster Hunter Rise
50 Stardew Valley, Plants vs. Zombies, Overcooked 2
52 Animal Crossing: New Horizons
54 Quiz: Name chooser

56 **Zelda games**
Intro and Link's Awakening
58 Breath of the Wild
60 Skyward Sword, Hyrule Warriors,
Retro Zelda
62 Quiz: Find your perfect Zelda

64 **Unmissable games**
Puzzle Games: Pikmin 3 Deluxe, Unravel Two
66 Platform Games: Sonic Mania, Rayman Legends
68 Battle Games: Splatoon 2, Super Bomberman R,
Mario + Rabbids Kingdom Battle
70 Battle Games: Super Smash Bros. Ultimate
72 Adventure Games: Miitopia, Kirby Star Allies,
Metroid Dread
74 Terraria, Hollow Knight
76 The ultimate Switch quiz
78 Quiz answers
79 Index
80 Ultimate Switch checklist

SECRETS OF THE SWITCH

The Switch is easy to use and packed full of fun—here's all you need to know to get started!

The Switch is very simple to set up on your TV—just plug it in and follow the instructions on screen. It comes with everything you need to play straight out of the box—and unlike some consoles, you don't even need to buy a second controller to play local multiplayer.

Strap yourself in

To use the Joy-Cons as two separate controllers, click the strap attachments into place. You can use the Joy-Cons without them, which is handy if you want to play a two-player game when you're traveling, but the bigger shoulder buttons on the attachments make the Joy-Cons easier to use. However, you can also buy larger holders to slot the Joy-Cons into, which make them like a small PlayStation controller. These are really worth getting—they make the Joy-Cons much less fiddly

Top Tip!

If you lose a Joy-Con, go to Controllers > Find Controllers on your Switch. You can make them vibrate to locate them!

More control

With so many great local multiplayer games, you may want to get more controllers to play four-player games at home. You can buy official Joy-Cons (these are essential if you want to play *Mario Party*), and if you buy different colors you can change up the look of your Switch. Or you can get yourself a Pro Controller, which is more like a traditional console controller. There are lots of controllers made by companies other than Nintendo. And if you've got another console, you can buy a widget that plugs into the Switch's USB port and allows you to use a PlayStation or Xbox controller on the Switch, which might save you some money!

Top Tip!
Screenshotting is easy on the Switch—press the square button on the left Joy-Con!

That's Mii

You can make a Mii (a little avatar that represents you) by going to System Settings > Mii. Most people make their Mii into a cartoon version of themselves, but you can make yours look any way you want. It can have bright green hair, if you like—maybe *you* have bright green hair! Some games let you bring your Mii into the action, like *Super Smash Bros. Ultimate*.

Customize your look!

Make your Mii just like you.

TAKE THE CASE

Get to grips with everything from protecting your Switch to purchasing downloads and archiving games.

If you're going to take your Switch outside your home—and we assume you will, because that's kind of the point—then a carry case is essential to protect it from damage. We also strongly advise getting a tempered glass screen protector! They're the same type you can use to protect phones and tablets, and while they can be tricky to fit (ask an adult do it), they're so worth it! It's easy to accidentally scratch your Switch when putting it in and taking it out of the dock, so put a protector on before you start using it, and keep that screen pristine.

Get connected

You can get a subscription to Switch Online, which you'll need for most online gaming. Free-to-play games like *Fortnite* and *Rocket League* work without it, but if you want to play *Minecraft* online, for instance, you'll need a subscription. You can also access a huge library of vintage NES and SNES games on Switch Online, as well as *Tetris 99*.

Top Tip!
If your battery keeps dying, try turning down the screen brightness!

Pokémon Sword & Shield, p37

Long term memory

You can either buy games on cartridges or download them from the Nintendo eShop. If you're planning on buying downloads, you'll need to expand your Switch's memory with a micro SD card. You don't have to buy an official Switch one—they cost more and are just the same as a normal one—so just make sure it's a good-quality card. Switch games generally don't take up as much space as PlayStation or Xbox games—very few are bigger than 20GB. For example, *Mario Kart 8 Deluxe* is under 7GB. So a card with at least 128GB of storage should keep you going.

Terraria, p74

Swap shop

There are pros and cons to cartridges and downloads. Downloads are instant, they're always on your console, and you can't lose them. But cartridges take up far less of your Switch's memory, and you can lend them to friends (who will *hopefully* lend you theirs in return!) or trade them in when you've finished with them.

Top Tip!

If you run out of storage, you can archive games—this deletes the game data while keeping your save data. You can re-download the game later.

Mario Kart 8 Deluxe, p20–21

Splatoon 2, p68

STORY OF THE SWITCH

Do you want to know more about how the Switch came to be? Read on...

Nintendo had great success with its Wii and DS consoles in the 2000s. The Wii's movement sensors gave its games an exciting new dimension, and the DS had seen off all its competitors to become the leading handheld console. However, the follow-up console, the Wii U, didn't do as well against the more powerful PS3 and Xbox One. Plus, the rise of smartphones meant players didn't need a separate console to play games on the go. What could Nintendo do about this?

The hybrid

Nintendo aimed to create a new gaming experience, combining things that had worked on previous systems, as well as some new ideas. The new console would have controllers that could be used as motion detectors, like the Wiimote, but could also be used as standard controllers or clipped together into one. It would have a touchscreen like the DS. But the most awesome new thing was that it could be used as a home console or a handheld. This gave the console its name—the Switch.

Did you know?

While it was in development, the Switch was codenamed "NX."

Nintendo has always been an innovative company, leading in new directions rather than following the crowd. Ever since the Wii, Nintendo aimed to offer something different to Sony and Microsoft's consoles, rather than competing with them head-on. The Switch focused on their strengths in handheld gaming, family-friendly games, and local multiplayer. And it packed a lot of power into its small frame—less than the PS4 and Xbox One, but still an impressive piece of equiptment.

Hit Switch

The Switch was unveiled on October 20, 2016 in a video that showed off its brilliant flexibility, and gamers all over the world were thrilled. It was released on March 3, 2017 and within a year over 14 million consoles had been sold—more than the Wii U had sold in its lifetime. On September 20, 2019 Nintendo released the Switch Lite, a handheld-only version. Sales of both types of Switch are now over 89 million. What a game-changer!

Did you know?

Nintendo keeps tweaking the Switch. Current models have a longer-lasting battery than the original version.

Super Smash Bros. Ultimate, p70

Super Mario Odyssey, p17

With so many games available, it can be hard to know what to play next. Take this test to find the perfect game for you...

1. What is your favorite color?

A Red
B Blue
C Green
D Yellow

2. What are you most likely to say?

A "I feel the need, the need for speed!"
B "I love puzzles!"
C "Will you be my friend?"
D "Who wants to go for a run?"

3. Which of the following best describes how you like to play?

A I love playing games with as many friends as possible.
B Solo gameplay, all the way!
C I don't like fighting games.
D I'd rather not sit down—I like an active game.

4. What's your favorite subject at school?

A Science. I'm super interested in how things work.
B History! It's so cool learning about the past.
C Geography because I love travel and exploring new places.
D PE—I'm all about the action!

5. What is your dream job?

A Racecar driver
B Archaeologist
C Travel agent
D Personal trainer

6. How would your friends describe you?

A Competitive and funny
B Brave and thoughtful
C Kind and considerate
D Full of energy and sporty

Mostly As

You should try Mario Kart 8 Deluxe. Hone your skills with some solo play, then invite your friends around for a multiplayer tournament or a manic *Balloon Battle*. Have a look on p20 for more details.

Mostly Bs

The Legend of Zelda: Breath of the Wild is definitely the game for you. Take your time and explore the vast landscape and puzzling shrines—just make sure you're tooled up with the right weapons. Turn to p58 to find out more.

Mostly Cs

Take some time out and take a trip to your own island in *Animal Crossing: New Horizons*. Gradually make friends with the cute and funny animals, while making your island as unique as you are. Find out more on p52.

Mostly Ds

Ring Fit Adventure is the perfect choice for gamers who are always on the go. With this game, you can get fit IRL while fighting monsters on the screen—double win! Turn to p42 for more about the game.

IT'S-A MARIO!

Everyone's favorite plumber really comes into his own on the Switch. If you don't have at least one Mario game in your collection, you're missing out!

From the multi-player competitiveness of *Mario Kart* to the single player adventures, there's a Mario game for every person and every mood. And you can even go old-school if you like and play some of the old NES and Super NES games with an online membership. The next few pages will give you the low-down on all the Mario games available on the Switch.

Mario Kart 8 Deluxe, p20-21

Did you know?

Mario first appeared on screen in 1981 as part of the game Donkey Kong.

Super Mario Odyssey, p17

16

Super Mario Odyssey

Star rating: ⭐⭐⭐⭐⭐

This is the ultimate Mario game for solo play, but you can also have fun with a friend—one of you as Mario and the other as his side-kick, Cappy. The game is so packed with quirky, fun characters and details, it won't be long before this living, thinking, talking hat feels like the most normal thing in the world! Time will fly as you leap about the different kingdoms, throwing Cappy at everyone and everything you see. This game ticks every box—awesome 3D play, gravity-defying moves, funny characters, retro sections, AND the occasional ability to stomp around as a T. rex in a hat… what's not to love?

Top Tip!
You don't always have to risk life and limb to collect coins—try tossing Cappy out and collecting them that way.

Dressed for success!

Make sure Mario is dressed appropriately—if it's hot, he needs to be protected from the sun, and if it's cold, wrap him up warm. When you've collected enough purple coins from a kingdom, head to the Crazy Cap store to buy the cap and outfit for the kingdom you are visiting. Put it on, and you should then be able to enter a locked door that leads to a Power Moon!

Mario Golf: Super Rush

Star rating:

Mario has been playing golf since the days of the NES—the sport is big in Japan and there are lots of video games aimed at making it simple and appealing to young players. It's been a long time since a *Mario Golf* game has been released for a home console, but the series is perfectly at home on the Switch because of its local multiplayer mode. It's OK as a single-player game, but the story mode is a bit short and there aren't many courses to play, so you may get bored with it pretty quickly. This game is best played with friends.

Top Tip!
Watch the weather—it makes a real difference to your shots!

Speed into battle

As well as playing standard golf on the courses, there are two other modes which offer something a little different. Speed Golf (which is a real thing!) sees players competing to finish a round in the quickest time—which is good if you have a friend or family member who takes forever on every shot. Battle Golf takes place on a big arena-style course with nine holes, and the first to sink a ball into three of them wins!

Super Mario 3D All-Stars

Star rating: ●●●●★

This collection brings together the flagship Mario games from three Nintendo consoles.

Galaxy quest

The best of the bunch is *Super Mario Galaxy*, a Wii game from 2007. In it, Mario bounces between tiny planets, asteroids, and space stations in search of the Power Stars. It feels bigger than any Mario game released up to that point, and jumping around in space is really exciting. Shame they didn't include *Super Mario Galaxy 2* though.

Top Tip!
Grab as many 1-Ups as you like in Comet Observatory. If you leave and come back, they respawn!

Sunshine days

Super Mario Sunshine, released on the Gamecube in 2002, has some problems with its camera, but it tries hard to do something different. In this game, Mario is tasked with cleaning up Isle Delfino, which has been covered in toxic slime, while the theft of its Shine Sprites has plunged it into darkness. Mario's water-squirting robot backpack FLUDD takes time to get used to, but is lots of fun.

When I'm 64

Super Mario 64 was originally released on the N64 in 1997, and was the first 3D *Mario* game. It was groundbreaking at the time, and does a good job of turning the familiar 2D Mario world into a much bigger and more open gameplay space, but its blocky graphics look pretty ugly now, and its camera can be really annoying.

Mario Kart 8 Deluxe

Star rating: ●●●●●

Ever since the first *Mario Kart* game in 1992, it's been one of the best reasons to own a Nintendo console. In all that time, no one has ever come close to matching it —it's probably the best local multiplayer game ever made, and great for all the family to play together. It's simple—you race and try to pick up special items like weapons and speed boosts. Every Nintendo console since the SNES has had a *Mario Kart* game, and *Mario Kart 8 Deluxe* is an upgrade on the Wii U's *Mario Kart 8*. It features 48 circuits, including retooled favourites from previous games. The gameplay is perfect (as we've come to expect), and its replay value is huge.

Top Tip!
The race leader gets weaker items, so watch out when you're winning!

Taking a shine

Battle Mode—a one-on-one game where you had to burst three balloons attached to your opponent's car—was a small part of the original *Super Mario Kart* that turned out to be a huge hit with players. *Mario Kart 8 Deluxe* has many more battle options—we like Shine Thief, where the winner is whoever can hang on to a Shine Sprite for 20 seconds. It doesn't sound like long, but it is when everyone's targeting you!

Stat attack

When choosing your rider, vehicle, wheels and glider, always click the plus button (or minus button, depending on which controller you're using) and check you're happy with your speed, acceleration, weight, grip, and handling. All of these things change when you alter any element of your set-up, and they'll all affect your race. We suggest you turn *off* tilt steering—using the stick is easier!

Top Tip!
Most circuits have shortcuts. See if you can find them!

Take it up a gear

Mario Kart Live: Home Circuit combines real remote-controlled cars with gameplay on the Switch. The cars have cameras, and you can race around real-world spaces while using the traditional *Mario Kart* items. And if that's not enough, throughout 2022 and 2023, 48 more courses will be released for *Mario Kart 8 Deluxe* through the Nintendo Switch Online + Expansion Pack membership or as a separate DLC.

Mario Tennis Aces

Star rating: ●●●●★

Nintendo's tennis games have come a long way since the original NES tennis, where Mario was the umpire. *Mario Tennis Aces* does for tennis what *Mario Kart* does for racing—it's an easy-to-play version of the sport that doesn't go for realism at all. Instead, you play as various Mario characters with wild and wacky skills, making it fun even if you're not a tennis fan. Tennis translates really well to video games—you can keep the entire court and all the players on screen at once, plus doubles makes a perfect local four-player game. Weirdly, there's also an adventure mode with a storyline, which doesn't really feel like something a tennis game needs—but it's a decent extra for a game whose main attraction is multiplayer fun.

Top Tip!
Aim a Zone Shot directly at your opponent to break their racket.

Mario and Sonic at the Olympic Games Tokyo 2020

Nintendo has released a Mario and Sonic crossover game to tie in with every Olympics since Beijing 2008. With the 2020 Games taking place in Japan, the birthplace of Mario and Sonic, this should have been the biggest one yet—but the event being delayed by a year stole its thunder. It's still a good entry in the series, with minigames based on various Olympic events, including a cute 8-bit style section set at Tokyo 1964 (which was long before the 8-bit era, but whatever). It's very much one to play with friends as the single-player modes are less fun.

Paper Mario: The Origami King

Star rating:

The original *Paper Mario*, released on the N64 in 2000, seemed like quite a random idea. You play as a paper cutout of Mario, walking through a 3D world. Why? Ultimately it didn't matter because the game was great—cleverly designed, simpler than the main *Mario* games, and with witty references to previous adventures. *The Origami King* brings all those qualities to the Switch! It has great storytelling, going from eerie to funny to sad, and its world is so much fun to explore. The combat system can get a bit annoying, though.

Top Tip!
Get free health top-ups by resting on benches!

25

Luigi's Mansion 3

Star rating: ⚪⚪⚪⚪⚪⚪

After years of playing second fiddle to his brother, Luigi finally got a starring role in the Gamecube ghost-hunting game *Luigi's Mansion*, and it has become a popular franchise in its own right. The third in the series might be the best yet, as Mario and friends are tricked into staying in a haunted hotel. It falls on Luigi to free them all from the clutches of King Boo, armed only with his ghost dog Polterpup and his ghost-sucking vacuum cleaner the Poltergust. There's so much to explore in the hotel! The elevator buttons are all missing, but once you find each one, you can return to that floor whenever you like.

Top Tip!
When you're up against two ghosts at once, try to suck them both in so the other doesn't attack you!

Multiplayer mansion

There are two different multiplayer modes that you can play locally or online. ScareScraper mode gives you a randomly generated building, and you must work together to clear it of ghosts. ScreamPark is a competitive mode— players get into two teams and play matches against each other.

RETRO MARIO

There are literally dozens of classic Mario games, and you can play several of them on your Switch if you subscribe to Switch Online.

NES

Donkey Kong is worth a play to see where it all began, but don't bother with the original *Mario Bros.*, as it's a pretty limited arcade game. Go direct to *Super Mario Bros.* It set the style for future Mario games. It's still fast, fun and challenging! *Super Mario Bros. 3* is just as good, and introduces the map-based RPG elements used in later games. The puzzler *Dr. Mario* is worth a try, but don't take medical advice from Mario; he's not a real doctor!

Top Tip!
Look out for the magic pink note block in World 1–3 of *Super Mario Bros. 3*!

SNES

Super Mario World was the launch game for the SNES and it's still one of the best in the series—the biggest platform game anyone had ever seen, with hidden levels to go back and explore even after you'd finished it. The follow-up, *Super Mario World 2: Yoshi's Island* is also a very fine game. The original *Super Mario Kart* was awesome for its time, but pales in comparison with *Mario Kart 8*.

N64

Paying extra for N64 gives you access to *Super Mario 64*, if you don't already have it on *3D All-Stars* —but we think the original *Paper Mario* stands up better today (ironically.) *Dr Mario 64* adds four-way multiplayer action to the original. The N64 edition of *Mario Tennis* is simpler than the more recent games.

With so many Marios to choose from, it's tricky to pick a favorite. Take this quiz to discover the perfect Mario for you!

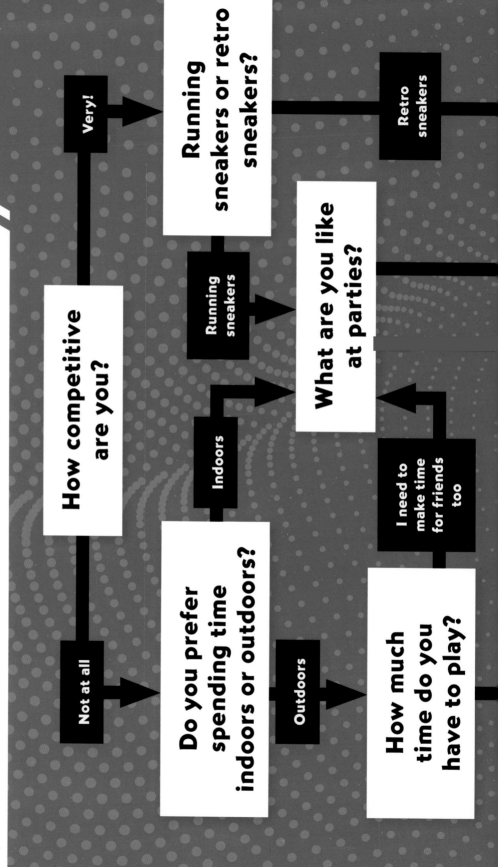

How competitive are you?

Very!

Not at all

Running sneakers or retro sneakers?

Retro sneakers

Running sneakers

Do you prefer spending time indoors or outdoors?

Indoors

Outdoors

What are you like at parties?

I need to make time for friends too

How much time do you have to play?

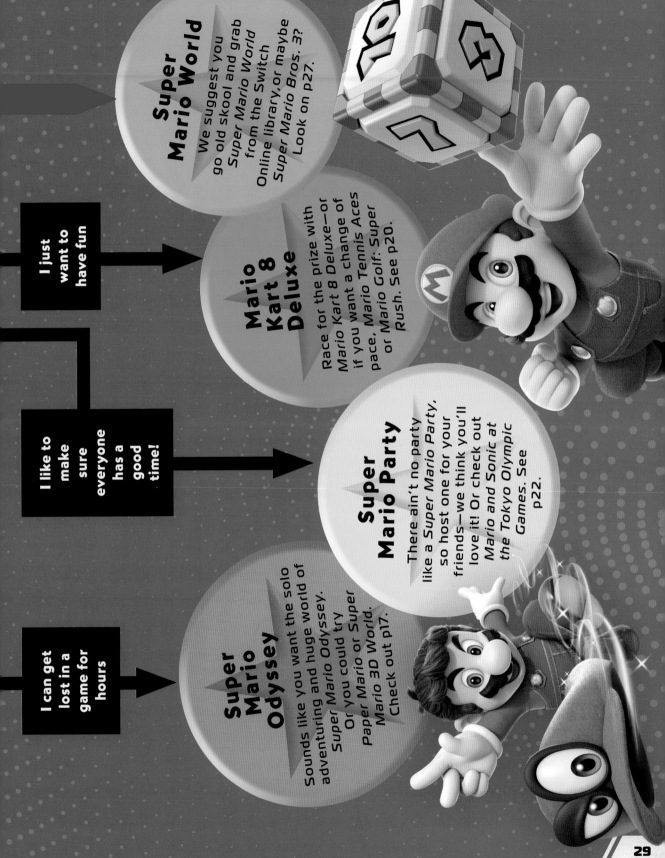

I just want to have fun

Super Mario World

We suggest you go old skool and grab from the Switch Online library, or maybe Super Mario Bros. 3? Look on p27.

Mario Kart 8 Deluxe

Race for the prize with Mario Kart 8 Deluxe—or if you want a change of pace, Mario Tennis Aces or Mario Golf: Super Rush. See p20.

I like to make sure everyone has a good time!

Super Mario Party

There ain't no party like a Super Mario Party, so host one for your friends—we think you'll love it! Or check out Mario and Sonic at the Tokyo Olympic Games. See p22.

I can get lost in a game for hours

Super Mario Odyssey

Sounds like you want the solo and huge world of adventuring Super Mario Odyssey. Or you could try Super Paper Mario or Super Mario 3D World. Check out p17.

SMALL BUT BEAUTIFUL

As gaming technology has advanced, it's become possible to make bigger and bigger games... but bigger isn't always better.

The rise of cheap downloadable games means small independent game studios can release small independent games since they don't have to pay to have loads of copies manufactured or fight for shelf space in the stores. Often, these indie games are quirkier, weirder, and more imaginative than big mainstream games.

Sale away

The only problem is there are tons of them, and not all of them are good. We've put together some recommendations here, but this is just a tiny sample of what's available. We suggest waiting until there's a sale at the Nintendo eShop, because you can pick up some huge bargains!

Among Us, p33

Untitled Goose Game

Star rating: ●●●●★

It's one of the quirkiest, funniest games around. *Untitled Goose Game* isn't the kind of thing you'd expect to be a hit game—it's set in a quiet English village, and you play as a mischievous goose. But everything about it is so well designed, from the puzzles you have to solve to the reactions of the villagers, that it's a complete joy to play. The goose can only do things an actual goose could do (it flaps, it honks, it picks up things in its beak), making the tasks even more challenging. It's a short game, but it's nice to get the satisfaction of finishing it in a couple of hours!

Shut your beak

Different villagers react differently to you—some let you approach, but others will chase you away. So don't draw extra attention to yourself by honking and flapping unless the task requires it (like when you have to chase the boy into the phone booth). Interfering villagers can be distracted by stealing their items and running away with them, but they'll be back before long!

Cuphead

This game is totally wild! Visually, it's designed to look like a 1930s cartoon (like the early Mickey Mouse shorts), and it really feels like playing through one of those cartoons. You might not know that if you've never seen one, but trust us, it does. Amazingly, the animations were drawn by hand rather than on computers! The game follows Cuphead and his brother Mugman as they travel around Inkwell Isle trying to pay off a gambling debt (there's a lesson there, kids). It's mostly a series of big enemy fights, and be warned... it gets tough!

Top Tip!
You have infinite lives in *Cuphead*, so don't worry about completing each stage the first time. Instead, learn how it works!

Night in the woods

Star rating:

This is a well-written, story-driven game with a weird, cool edge to it. You play as Mae Borowski, a college dropout who's returned to her small hometown of Possum Springs. She tries to get to grips with how the town has changed while she's been away... and eventually learns its terrible secret. There's a nice mix of adventure, spooky exploration, and just hanging out! There are dozens of characters, and the ones you choose to spend time with affect how your game develops.

Among Us

Star rating: ⚫⚫⚫⚫⭐

This multiplayer game was a hit on Steam and the Switch was the first console to get it. It's based on the party game *Mafia* and is similar to a lot of "murder mystery" games on *ROBLOX*, but it's really well designed. The players are astronauts in a ship or a base (there are different maps to play), and one or more of them are secretly murderers. The murderer(s) must kill off the other crewmembers without being suspected. The crew hold votes to decide who they're going to throw out of the airlock, hoping to get rid of the murderer.

Top Tip!

If you're a Crewmate, don't just focus on finding the Impostor(s)—you can also win by completing the tasks!

Strong support

Like a lot of online multiplayer games, the fun of *Among Us* is that every game is slightly different. Players have strategies and it's hard to tell whether you're up against a bunch of geniuses or a bunch of noobs. The developer, Innersloth, was going to release a sequel, but cancelled it to focus on upgrading the original game.

POKÉMON GAMES

Find out how Pokémon has adapted and grown with ever-changing technology to become what it is today!

Pokémon was built for handheld gaming—the first games in the series came out on the Game Boy Color back in 1996, and it was years before a Pokémon game was released on a home console. That's because, in the days before online gaming, there was no way of linking two home consoles together. But you could link two Game Boys, so you were able to trade Pokémon with your friends and battle each other.

The adventure of linking

This means Pokémon has really come into its own in the online gaming era! You don't need a cable to link your Switch to a friend's, so trading and battling is much easier. Plus the current crop of Pokémon games are better than ever. Like so many of the great Nintendo games, these are about exploring a fantasy world—in this case, discovering strange creatures and training them to fight each other.

Pokémon Sword & Shield, p37

New Pokémon Snap, p39

Pokémon Sword & Shield

Star rating: ⊘⊘⊘⊘⊘

These entries in the *Pokémon* series are set in Galar, which is based on the United Kingdom. The attention to detail in the design and characterization is really impressive. It feels like stepping into an episode of the cartoon series—in fact, it looks better! The gameplay will be familiar to anyone who's played a *Pokémon* game before. You play a trainer just starting out in the world, gifted a starter Pokémon by star trainer Leon. With it you battle and capture other Pokémon and gain experience, working toward competing in tournaments. But this game introduces a new idea—the Wild Area, which is an open-world section where you can take time out from the main storyline.

Top Tip!
Update your Player Card regularly at Pokémon Centers as it doesn't automatically update.

Sword or Shield?

The difference between the two games is that *Sword* features the legendary Pokémon Zamazenta, while *Shield* features Zacian—everything else is the same. You can transfer Pokémon from *Pokémon Go* and the *Let's Go* games, but only if they're included in the *Sword* and *Shield* Pokédex, because not every Pokémon is featured in the game. This decision didn't go down well with everyone! But the *Pokémon* games are always high quality and these continue that tradition.

Pokémon: Let's Go Pikachu! & Let's Go, Eevee!

Star rating: ⚪⚪⚪⚪★

The mobile game *Pokémon Go* was the first Pokémon game not to be released on a Nintendo system —and since it's free to play, it's brought in many new fans. The *Let's Go!* games are aimed at those gamers. They are actually remakes of one of the earliest games in the series, the Game Boy Color game *Pokémon Yellow*. And as the first Pokémon games for the Switch, they were the first Pokémon games on a home console. They're a great way into the wider world of Pokémon, very accessible to new players. Plus, the fact you can connect it with *Pokémon Go* is a major bonus.

Top Tip!

Unlike *Pokémon Go*, where wild Pokémon only flee after breaking free of a Pokéball, in *Let's Go* they can flee at any time—so throw quickly!

Pokémon Legends: Arceus

Star rating: ⚪⚪⚪⚪★

This game is a major evolution of the Pokémon series. Set in the past, at a time when Pokémon weren't as well understood as they are now, you play a new researcher helping to compile the first-ever Pokédex. Whereas previous games focused on training and battling, *Arceus* is much more about exploring an open world and catching Pokémon. You can choose which research tasks you do to complete a Pokédex entry, so you can play the game your way. It takes a little while to get going, but this could be the future of Pokémon.

Pokémon Unite

Sure, *Pokémon* is great, but haven't you always wished it was more like *Rocket League*? No? Well, that's what you get with *Pokémon Unite*. In this free-to-play multiplayer online game, you join a team of five trainers and play matches against others. The aim of the game is to battle other Pokémon in the arena, pick up the balls they drop after being knocked out and dunk the ball into the opponents' goal (it's more like a basketball hoop.) It's weird, but fun, and free! (It's also available on phones and tablets.)

Top Tip!
Look out for the yellow monster icons on the map—they indicate a new, powerful Pokémon has appeared, which you can beat and recruit for your team!

New Pokémon Snap

Top Tip!
Turning from one side to the other is pretty slow, but you can change the camera speed!

This is such a clever idea—you become a wildlife photographer, but for Pokémon. You embark on a series of nature trails in the Lental region and try to get some good shots of wild Pokémon. When you return, you select your best pictures and present them to Professor Mirror. The Professor then judges your photos based on how centered the subject is, what pose they're in, how close you've managed to get, and if you've captured any unusual behaviour. It's a gentle alternative to more competitive Pokémon games, and weirdly addictive as you try to improve your photography skills.

GAME SELECTOR

Find your perfect Pokémon game by completing this fun quiz! Ready, set... go!

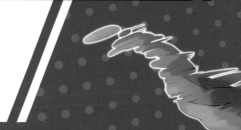

1. What's your favorite thing to do in Pokémon?

A Talk to other trainers
B Complete the Pokédex
C Interact with Pokémon
D Battle!

2. Where would you like to go on vacation?

A Around the United Kingdom
B Japan
C An island in the Pacific
D Don't mind; as long as I'm with friends!

3. What's your favorite school subject?

A Geography
B Biology
C Art
D PE

4. Would you like to be famous?

A Only if I felt I deserved it
B I'd prefer go under the radar
C I'd rather just do something I'm proud of
D Totally!

5. Do you like spending time in nature?

A Yes
B Sometimes—I like to change it up
C It's the best!
D Nope!

6. Choose your favorite Pokémon from these options:

A Scorbunny
B Eevee
C Torterra
D Charizard

Mostly Bs

We suggest *Pokémon Let's Go, Pikachu!* or *Let's Go, Eevee!*, which offer straight-up traditional Pokémon action. See p38.

Mostly As

Go for *Pokémon Sword & Shield*, with its strong storyline, large cast of characters, and open-world wild area. See p37.

Mostly Cs

Get a different experience with *New Pokémon Snap* and take a Pokémon safari. See p39.

Mostly Ds

Try all-out battle in *Pokémon Unite*, the sports multiplayer game for Pokémon! See p39.

GET-UP-AND-GO GAMES

Ring Fit Adventure

Star rating: ⚪⚪⚪⚪⭐

The Wii established Nintendo as the place to go for active games: *Wii Fit* and *Wii Sports* are still in the top ten bestselling games of all time, and *Wii Sports* is the bestselling Nintendo game ever, on any system. The Switch's motion-based controls have attracted less attention than the Wii's, but they're still an important part of the console. Nintendo has taken the "exergame" to a new level with *Ring Fit Adventure*, livening up your exercise routine with a simple role-playing game.

Lord of the ring

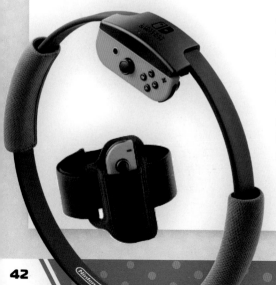

Ring Fit Adventure comes with two attachments for your Joy-Cons: the Ring-Con, which has a space for you to slot one Joy-Con into, and a leg strap, which means the other Joy-Con can keep track of your leg movements. In the game, you team up with a Ring to battle a bodybuilding dragon named Dragaux and his minions. You have to run and use the Ring-Con to jump and shoot: When you fight a monster, the game goes into turn-based combat mode. Perform an exercise well, and you'll deal damage! Now that's what we call a power workout.

Cut to the chase

Don't expect anything too challenging from the RPG storyline—this is designed for people who don't play a lot of games. The focus is really on the exercise; the story just makes it more fun. Of course, you may have a parent who's interested in using the Switch to exercise but doesn't want to bother with the RPG stuff. For them, there's a mode where you just do the exercises—and though there's no multiplayer mode, you can compete against each other by taking turns doing the exercises, like a fitness-based version of *Super Mario Party*. There's also a Rhythm Mode in the style of *Just Dance*.

Top Tip!
Food items play an important role in *Ring Fit Adventure*—they can make the difference between winning and losing battles!

Extra motivation

The good thing about the RPG storyline is that it keeps things interesting. Fitness games can get repetitive if you're doing the same things in the same virtual locations all the time, but *Ring Fit Adventure* takes you to new places and unlocks new things. And where other fitness games give you a trash score for doing badly, here you can be defeated by a monster! It all encourages you to play often and play well.

Just Dance

This ever-popular series is pretty self-explanatory—you just dance. It's really well suited to the Joy-Cons—you can just hold them in your hands, or buy wrist straps. Like *FIFA*, the game is updated each year with only minor changes to the gameplay, and whereas *FIFA* updates the players, *Just Dance* features a new set of tracks to dance to. You can also pay for a subscription that unlocks a much bigger library of tracks—though this seems a little outrageous when the game isn't cheap in the first place.

Top Tip!
Dance five times to any track to unlock an alternate version of it!

Fitness Boxing 2: Rhythm And Exercise

The *Fitness Boxing* games are exclusive to the Switch, because they're really based around the dual Joy-Cons—you hold one in each fist and punch in time to the music. The track selection in both games is pretty good, easily as good as the *Just Dance* games. It gives you a decent workout, but there isn't much variety and the motion detection isn't always accurate. The second in the series includes a two-player mode, but please don't punch each other for real.

Arms

This fun fighting game can be used with the Joy-Con motion controls or normal button controls—but it's most fun with the Joy-Cons! Your fighters have extendable arms, which you can use to punch, block, and throw your opponent—and the arms are detachable, so you can choose different arms for each battle and unlock new arms, too. It's all ridiculously fun, especially in one of the multiplayer modes.

Top Tip!
Remember: Punches beat throws, throws get past blocks, blocks stop punches.

Carnival Games

This is a *Mario Party*-style collection of minigames based on the kind of things you'd play at a carnival or arcade—throw the basketball in the hoop, throw a hoop over a bottle, plus other games not involving hoops. It's a little bit smaller and more limited than *Super Mario Party*, and it seems odd that you have to beat each minigame to unlock the motion-controlled version—but it's still a nice alternative if you've played all the Mario minigames to death.

CROSS-PLATFORM CLASSICS

Minecraft

Star rating:

The bestselling video game *of all time* is more than a decade old and just keeps on going! Lots of stuff has been added into *Minecraft* in that time, but underneath it's the same game it's always been—and it's the creative possibilities that keep players coming back. It's an awesomely simple open-world game where you mine, build, and survive—and you don't even have to do the survival part, because there's a creative mode where you can just build in peace with unlimited materials. Everyone should try it!

Top Tip!
The best level to look for diamonds is Y-11—activate "show coordinates" in game settings to find it.

Minecraft Dungeons

Star rating:
⬤ ⬤ ⬤ ★ ★

This RPG spin-off from Minecraft is a story-based game that takes place in the Minecraft world. It's not about mining and building—you adventure through dungeons, slay monsters, dodge traps, solve puzzles, and look for treasure. It doesn't have the creative aspect of the original game, but it's a lot of fun!

FIFA

The world's favorite soccer game is available on all consoles and is updated every year—its range of officially licensed leagues and clubs is unbeatable. However, the Switch version has often been criticized for offering fewer features than the PlayStation and Xbox editions. If you want a straight soccer game, *FIFA* does the job—and it works better on Switch than it did on the Wii or Wii U. But if you own a non-Nintendo console, it's better to buy it on that.

Top Tip!
Don't sprint everywhere all the time! It tires your players out and makes ball control harder.

Rocket League

Star rating:

It's soccer played with rocket-powered cars! You have to crash into the ball with your car—the ball is huge, the goals are huge, but getting the ball to go where you want is far from easy. It's really frustrating but weirdly addictive. The classic format involves two teams of three, and you can play locally or against bots. But it's the online multiplay that made this game a global hit—and it went free-to-play in 2020, which makes it a must-have for any Switch gamer.

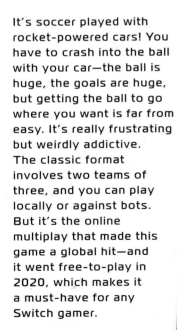

Top Tip!
Master quick turns with the power slide—hold down L2!

Fortnite

Star rating: ○○○○○

The world's favorite Battle Royale game is another free-to-play, online multiplayer game. A hundred players are dropped onto an island and are pushed together as a deadly storm closes in. You must grab weapons, find supplies—and eliminate everyone else until you're the last one alive! The game runs in seasons, with new gameplay elements and locations to keep things interesting. Buying a Battle Pass adds to the fun, and you can pay for skins and other items—but you can't buy weapons or anything else that'll help you win a match! Which is good—everyone starts off equal, and you can't win by being rich.

Top Tip!
The essential weapon in the game is the assault rifle! Even a common assault rifle is worth carrying.

Dodge the crowds

Fortnite can be brutal and bewildering at first—a lot of players jump out of the Battle Bus that flies over the island the first chance they get, and a lot of players get eliminated before they even find a weapon. If you're a *Fortnite* noob, stay on the bus until the last moment, and try to land away from other players—give yourself a chance to prepare before you meet anyone!

Hades

This is what's known as a "dungeon crawler" game, where the hero must fight their way through room after room of enemies and try not to die. *Hades* has a neat twist, because its hero, Zagreus, is trying to escape the underworld of Greek mythology, which is the land of the dead—so every death sends him back where he came from. You can also earn upgrades and new abilities to help you on the next run, so you're making progress even when you're fighting through the same rooms over and over again. A lot of the fun is in the characters you meet on the way, who try to help or hinder you.

Top Tip!
Don't waste money on items early in the game—save it for when you get a chance to buy rare items!

Monster Hunter Rise

The latest game in the *Monster Hunter* series has similar gameplay to previous ones: You hunt monsters, slay or capture them, and then get rewards. The big difference is that the map now has more physical depth to it, so you can move up and down much more—that's where the "Rise" part comes in. Even more excitingly, you can be joined on your quest by an animal. The Palicoes, which are basically cats, have featured in previous games, but *Rise* adds Palamutes, which will appeal to dog lovers.

Top Tip!
Always talk to Hinoa the Quest Maiden before setting out, and fill out your optional subquests.

Stardew Valley

Star rating: ⬤⬤⬤⬤⬤

Most games these days are put together by huge teams of developers—coders, artists, animators, writers, musicians and many more. Not *Stardew Valley*, which was entirely made by Eric "ConcernedApe" Barone. Inspired by the *Harvest Moon* series which had been popular on the DS, he wanted to make a game based around living in a small rural community—farming, chatting to the townspeople, collecting rare items, and facing the dangers lurking in the mines. The graphics look like something that might have been on the SNES, but the gameplay has its own gentle vibe. It's well-suited to the Switch—some games are better played at home, while others are better for playing while travelling, but *Stardew Valley* is definitely both.

Top Tip!
The Traveling Cart sells random items, often outside their usual seasons, and can be found in Cindersap Forest—but only on Fridays and Sundays!

Games within games

Inside the Stardrop Saloon are two arcade machines. *Journey of the Prairie King* is a Western-themed game similar to the 1979 Nintendo arcade game, *Sheriff* (one of the company's first big successes); *Junimo Kart*, which can be unlocked with the Skull Key, requires you to steer a cart past obstacles. Beat either game, and you'll get your own arcade machine for your home!

Plants vs. Zombies: Battle For Neighborville

The *Plants vs. Zombies* series has been a strong favourite for years, and this is the first one that's available for Switch. It's a simple concept: there's a zombie apocalypse raging, and the only ones who can protect us are plants. Players control either the plants or the zombies, and there are competitive and cooperative multiplayer modes. There aren't any great surprises here if you've played previous *Plants vs. Zombies* games, but it's good, silly fun all the same.

Overcooked 2

Restaurant kitchens are really stressful places to work, with loads of things going on at once, impatient customers waiting at their tables, and no room for error. So why not experience that stress with your friends and family? That's the concept behind the *Overcooked* games. It really is super stressful—and you will have arguments—but it's also one of the best multiplayer co-op games around. *Overcooked 2* introduces online multiplayers with a matchmaking feature, so that you can get annoyed with complete strangers!

New arrivals

Also, check out the cutesome battle royale game *Fall Guys*; the first open-world *Sonic* game, *Sonic Frontiers*, which takes inspiration from *Zelda*; and *Lego Star Wars: The Skywalker Saga*, where you can play through nine *Star Wars* movies in Lego form.

Animal Crossing: New Horizons

Star rating: ●●●●●

The *Animal Crossing* series dates way back to the N64. It's basically a cuter, more chilled version of 'social simulation' games like *The Sims*: you set up a home, do things to earn money, spend the money on clothes and stuff for your home and interact with other people. It's open-ended, and you can do pretty much what you like! Time in the game goes by at the same speed as it does in real life, which gives it a nice, relaxed feel. *New Horizons*, the fifth game in the series, might be the best yet—it came out just as many countries were telling everyone to stay at home due to Covid-19, and it was the ideal game to play when stuck indoors.

Island life

Why is it called *New Horizons*? Well, previous *Animal Crossing* games have all been set in villages that already existed before you got there, but this time, you're part of a plan to set up home on a deserted island. You and two NPCs pitch your tents and start developing the island—and the other two are immediately impressed with you, so you're basically in charge. You can play local and online multiplayer, so you can develop your island with friends—and you can invite other players to visit!

Learn to earn

Practically everything you do in *New Horizons* earns rewards, whether in the form of Bells (the in-game currency) or NookMiles. Tom Nook, who runs the *New Horizons* island, issues reward cards—collect stamps on these cards to earn NookMiles, which can be used to pay off your moving expenses, build a new home or buy special items. Timmy Nook will buy pretty much anything from you, from furniture to insects. We do wonder what he does with all those grasshoppers, though. Maybe he eats them like in *Survivor!*

Top Tip!

If you craft items into tools or furniture before selling them, you'll get more money!

Second homes

A DLC add-on for *New Horizons*, *Happy Home Paradise*, was released in late 2021 and focuses on the designing aspect of the game. You get to take on other islanders as clients and design holiday homes for them, after listening to what they want, and you get paid in a new currency called Poki. It's not worth it if you're not that interested in design—but if you are, it's great fun trying out different looks that you'd never use for your own home, but which fit another character perfectly. It really refreshes the game, and devoted *Animal Crossing* fans should definitely check it out.

Which Switch character are you? Answer these questions to see if you're most like Tom Nook, Alex, Steve, Kirby, or Peely!

1. Where would you most like to live?

A On an island
B In a valley
C In the sky
D Who cares? It's gonna get destroyed anyway.

2. How do you feel about giving people money?

A Of course, yes, yes! But I'll need you to pay it back.
B OK, but I worked pretty hard for that, you know…
C I'll give people whatever they need!
D You'll have to kill me for it.

3. What do you like to do on your days off?

A I don't take days off—someone might need me!
B A little DIY and maybe take a nap
C Spend it with friends
D Camp out and watch for my enemies

4. What's your greatest fear?

A That people will be unhappy
B Zombies, skeletons, etc
C That the universe will be destroyed
D I don't fear anything!

5. What would you like to be as a grown-up?

A A real estate agent
B An architect
C A team leader
D A banana

6. Choose a color:

A Brown
B Green
C Pink
D Yellow

Mostly As

You are **Tom Nook** from *Animal Crossing*. He's always there to help, but business is business! Yes!

Mostly Bs

You are **Steve or Alex** from *Minecraft*. If you want anything, you're ready to work for it!

Mostly Cs

You are **Kirby** from *Kirby Star Allies*. You're super sociable and can make friends with anyone.

Mostly Ds

You are **Peely** from *Fortnite*. You're a banana with a gun. Good going...

ZELDA GAMES

Which version of Zelda is your top pick? Read on to learn what sparks your imagination, and get playing!

Mario may be the flagship brand of Nintendo, but the *Legend of Zelda* series is just as good—maybe better—in terms of the quality of the games. The first was released for the NES in 1986 and offered a Japanese take on sword-and-sorcery stories like *The Lord of the Rings*. It combined exploration, combat, puzzles, and interaction with other characters. Shigeru Miyamoto—who also created Mario—came up with the idea because he wanted kids in cities to have experiences like he had, wandering in the countryside. Since then, there have been more than 20 games in the series.

Link's Awakening, p57

The whole saga

The *Legend of Zelda* games take place in a very different order to when they were released, and some of them happen in parallel universes. It's all somewhat confusing, and you don't need to follow it to play the games. But if you want to play all the ones playable on the Switch in order, it goes: *Skyward Sword*, *A Link to the Past*, *Link's Awakening*, *The Legend of Zelda*, *The Adventure of Link*, and *Breath of the Wild*.

Did you know?

Zelda was named after the American writer and painter Zelda Fitzgerald.

The Legend Of Zelda: Link's Awakening

Star rating: ⬤⬤⬤⬤⬤

The original *Link's Awakening* from 1993 was one of the best Game Boy games of all time—so Nintendo decided to give it a complete remake for the Switch, getting rid of the green-screen graphics from the original and bringing in a whole new cute style. Although the new graphics are 3D and fully animated, it keeps the layout of the original game— which means a classic *Zelda* overhead view and a one-screen-at-a-time movement. It offers a change of pace from *Breath of the Wild*, and its simpler arrangement makes it a great game to play on the go.

Dungeon master

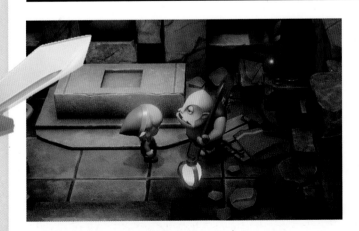

One major new element of the Switch version of *Link's Awakening* is Chamber Dungeons, a *Super Mario Maker*-style dungeon-builder. As you complete the game's dungeons, you can collect rooms that you can use to make your own dungeons. Go to Dampé's shack, and you'll not only be able to build dungeons, you can complete them to earn rewards.

The Legend of Zelda: Breath of the Wild

Star rating: ⬤⬤⬤⬤⬤

Originally developed for the Wii U, *Breath of the Wild* took so long to make it got delayed by two years—so Nintendo decided to make it a launch game for the Switch to give the new console a boost. And it really worked! A lot of people have called it the best *Zelda* game of all, maybe the best game of all time, making it one of the best reasons to buy a Switch.

Memory test

At the beginning of *Breath of the Wild*, Link has been asleep in a healing chamber for a hundred years and has lost his memory. The Kingdom of Hyrule has seen better days, and much of it is in ruins—and it's coming under threat from Ganon, an evil Calamity, who's been building his strength while sealed in Hyrule Castle. Link must regain his past and defeat Ganon… and if you collect all 13 images on the Captured Memories quest, you can unlock a secret ending.

Taking flight

You'll start the game on the Great Plains, and it can take a good couple of hours just to reach the point where you acquire the paraglider. Getting this allows you to access the rest of the map, and then the game *really* begins. When you reach Kakariko Village, it's a smart move to get some new clothes, especially something warmer so that you can cope with snowy conditions.

Big, wide world

The *Zelda* games are famous for their open-world approach, but *Breath of the Wild* takes this further than ever, with a huge map and plenty of side quests (76, to be precise). Want to focus on defeating Ganon and completing the whole story? Go for it! Just want to wander around looking for ingredients and learning recipes? That's cool, too! Most games have areas that you can't actually reach—they're part of the landscape but not part of the game—but in *Breath of the Wild*, you can climb pretty much any surface and explore anywhere. Since the map is so big, it's a good idea to activate the shrines that you come across—once activated, you can use them to teleport to each other, which saves a *lot* of time.

The Legend of Zelda: Skyward Sword HD

Star rating: ⬤⬤⬤⬤★

Skyward Sword was originally released on the Wii in 2011. It's a really important installment in the *Legend of Zelda* series—it's set before all the other games and sees Link complete his knight training. It's also very different to other *Zelda* games. Whereas *Breath of the Wild* is all about exploration, *Skyward Sword* is a much more story-based game, guiding the player from place to place. When it first came out, some people didn't think it felt *Zelda*-y enough—and not everyone was a big fan of how the Wii's unusual control system worked with the game. This HD remaster for the Switch can't completely fix the control problems, but it reveals that *Skyward Sword* is actually a great game in its own way.

One for newbies

Some gamers who've never played a *Zelda* game before might feel a little overwhelmed by *Breath of the Wild*—it's so huge and you don't get much guidance. So *Skyward Sword HD* may be a better place to start—as well as being set at the beginning of the Link and Zelda saga, it's an easier game to get into. It's also awesomely designed: The upscaled graphics look excellent, and the characters are brought to life so well that it's a very memorable experience.

Hyrule Warriors: Age of Calamity

This crossover between *Zelda* and *Dynasty Warriors* is more combat-based than normal *Zelda* games—this kind of game is known as "hack and slash," where you get attacked by large numbers of enemies and have to hack your way past them. It's a sequel to a popular Wii U game (which is also available on Switch), and it slots nicely into the world created by *Breath of the Wild*, even though it's not a "proper" *Zelda* game. The combat system is well worked out, and there's something very satisfying about pulling off a successful move.

Retro Zelda

The NES library on Switch Online has the first two *Zelda* games. They're very different from the detailed worlds you may be used to seeing—in the first game, *The Legend of Zelda*, the map is divided up into screens. It's a 2D landscape viewed from above, so there's no jumping or climbing. The second, *The Adventure of Link*, moves between an overhead map and more conventional 8-bit side-scrolling levels.

Their worlds do feel really big, and it's a challenge just to remember where everything is—the dungeons are especially fun. The SNES library offers *A Link to the Past*, which returns to the overhead view. It's a similar game to the original but is a little more advanced and has more depth. It's still regularly cited as one of the greatest games ever made, so it's worth trying!

New arrivals

How do you expand on a game like *Breath of the Wild*? By going upward! The sequel to *Breath of the Wild*, due in 2022, partly takes place in the skies above Hyrule.

YOUR PERFECT ZELDA GAME

Which version of Zelda matches your own personality? Answer the questions in the fun quiz below to find out! Happy playing…

How do you like to plan your day?

I always have a backup plan!

I go with the flow

What superpower would you have?

Super strength

Time travel

Do you prefer to focus on one thing?

Find one thing and keep doing it

No, I like doing lots of different things

Which animal do you prefer?

History

What kind of book would you most like to receive as a present?

A Link to the Past

You might enjoy the split timelines of retro SNES adventure *A Link to the Past*. See p61.

Hyrule Warriors

You're best suited to the heavy battle action of *Hyrule Warriors*—all fighting, all the time. See p61.

Skyward Sword HD

Try *Skyward Sword HD*, a narrative-based game that brings you right back to the beginning of Link's story. See p60.

Breath of the Wild

Go for *Breath of the Wild*, a detailed on-the-ground adventure with lots of climbing. See p58.

Bear

Eagle

Cookery

Pikmin 3 Deluxe

Star rating:

The original *Pikmin* game on the Gamecube was designed by Shigeru Miyamoto, one of the great geniuses of computer games—he also created *Mario* and *Zelda*, so not a bad track record. The main characters of this third game in the series are three space captains who land on another planet and befriend the native species, the Pikmin. The aim is to find fruit seeds that will save the captains' home planet from famine.

Pik and Choose

Your Pikmin are like a little army—they have different abilities, and it's up to you to decide how to use them to achieve whatever needs to be done on each level, such as getting around an obstacle or defeating an enemy. What's great about *Pikmin* is it's a puzzle game with real heart—it's got all the addictiveness of games where you move shapes around or match colors, but you also get really attached to the little characters. The main story isn't that long, but it's satisfying to keep working on your strategy.

Top Tip!
If a Pikmin is drowning or on fire, blow your whistle to keep them from panicking!

Unravel Two

Star rating: ⬤⬤⬤⬤⬤

Everything about this game is just beautiful. As with the original *Unravel*, you play as a Yarny, a small creature made of yarn who's been shipwrecked on an island. But this sequel adds another dimension—it's joined by another lost Yarny, and together they explore the island and get past obstacles. They can unravel their yarn, swing from it, make bridges from it, lasso objects using it, and use it to pull each other up.

Top Tip!
If you're unsure that something will work, send one Yarny ahead to try it—then if you fall, the other Yarny can pull them back up.

It takes two

Many of the puzzles are based around the two Yarnys working together, but the game works just as well in solo or two-player mode—you press "X" to switch between them when playing solo or take one each if playing two-player. One Yarny can also carry the other to speed things up. The controls are excellent—once you've figured out what you need to do, getting the timing right is pretty easy. As you progress, a storyline develops that is surprisingly serious for a game about two little beings made of yarn.

Sonic Mania

Star rating:

One of the biggest game series of the 1990s, *Sonic the Hedgehog* was possibly the best 2D platformer of all time: You played as the superfast blue hedgehog, making your way through bright-colored worlds, collecting rings and fighting robotized animals. But while the *Mario* series moved smoothly into the era of 3D gaming, *Sonic* always struggled—its speed and awesomely simple attack system became clumsy and annoying. So the makers of *Sonic Mania* decided to go for a retro 2D style, with superb results. There are lots of new elements, but it's very much the same old *Sonic*. If you're used to modern games, beware: This is a 90s-style game, and it's *very* easy to die!

Top Tip!

The bosses at the end of each act have an attack pattern—learn it, and watch for an opportunity to strike back!

Level up

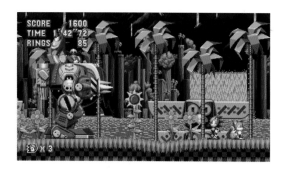

Sonic Mania features remixed and expanded versions of eight zones from classic *Sonic* games, along with four brand-new zones and the fiendish bonus stages from *Sonic 3* and *Sonic CD* both feature. To fully complete the game, you need to find the giant rings that lead to the "chase the spaceship" special stages and collect the chaos emeralds!

Rayman Legends

Star rating: ⬤⬤⬤⬤⬤

Rayman has been around almost as long as Sonic, but where Sonic struggled to live up to his great early games, *Rayman Legends* has been hailed as maybe the best of the bunch. Rayman himself is a little guy with no neck, arms, or legs, but his head, hands, and feet are attached floatingly to his body. This means that he can perform unusual moves like "throwing" his fists and spinning his head. In *Rayman Legends,* our hero awakes from a hundred years' sleep to find five Dark Teensies threatening the land—he must defeat them and rescue the Teensies... all **826** of them!

Top Tip!
After completing a tricky stage, consider taking a second run at it to hone your skills— and collect more Teensies—before moving on.

Legendary friends

Rayman Legends has a four-way co-op mode, allowing all the players to make their way through the levels at the same time. But the game is a fantastic experience in any mode, because the levels are so inventive and there is a lot of variety. The multiplayer football minigame, *Kung Foot,* is a great little feature, too. Legendary friends for sure!

BATTLE GAMES

Splatoon 2

Star rating: ⚪⚪⚪⚪⭐

Splatoon is a perfect example of how the Wii U had plenty of great games, but they weren't big hits because not enough people owned a Wii U. When the sequel was released on the Switch, it was massive! It's a simple enough idea—it is paintballing, except that players can also turn into squids and swim through their team's ink—but the design is so good. Tons of work went into the characters and their clothing.

Top Tip!
Though the main appeal of *Splatoon 2* is multiplayer, the Story Mode is great and gives you lots of training!

Online only

The only problem with *Splatoon 2* is that there's no local multiplayer. True, this kind of battle game works best when your opponents can't see what you're up to—but surely the co-op modes would be perfectly suited to playing on one screen? This would be so good as a family game, but unfortunately, only households with more than one Switch can do this! Time to get some Switch-owning friends over.

Super Bomberman R

Star rating:

The *Bomberman* series has been a mainstay of Nintendo consoles since the NES, and the gameplay hasn't really changed that much. It's a combination of battle and puzzle game—you're in an arena filled with obstacles, enemies, and immovable rocks, and you must plant bombs to break walls and destroy enemies—without blowing yourself up. It's like a more tactical version of *Pac-Man*. The Switch version is a little more complex, and its multiplayer mode is great, allowing you to blow each other up. There's also a free-to-play Battle Royale version, *Super Bomberman R Online*.

Top Tip!

New *Bomberman* players often just bash that bomb button—don't! You'll do much better if you place bombs carefully.

Mario + Rabbids Kingdom Battle

Star rating:

This crossover between *Mario* and the *Raving Rabbids* series is a turn-based battle game, a little like tabletop wargames. The Rabbids have brought chaos to the Mushroom Kingdom, and it's up to Mario and friends (plus four Rabbids dressed as other *Mario* characters) to win it back. It's all about strategy—you need to decide how to take the kingdom back—but there are lots of different types of gameplay here, such as puzzles to win new items. The co-op multiplayer adds replay value.

New arrivals

Mario + Rabbids Sparks of Hope, releasing in 2022, features more open levels and introduces Rabbid Rosalina.

Super Smash Bros. Ultimate

Star rating: ⚪⚪⚪⚪⚪

As well as being one of the best one-on-one "beat 'em up" games ever, *Super Smash Bros.* is a celebration of all things Nintendo, with characters and settings from across the company's titles. At first, its furious action can be hard to keep track of, and you'll probably get badly beaten in your first few matches—especially if you're playing against a friend who hasn't told you anything about how it works. But once you start picking up the mechanics of combat, the game quickly becomes addictive—especially in multiplayer, where the losing player will instantly want revenge. It's a classic you'll keep coming back to.

Top Tip!
Fighting regular battles is the quickest way to unlock characters—the story mode takes a while to complete.

Get set

You don't have to just go with the default settings—you can tweak all aspects of the rules, from which items drop to whether the winner needs a knockout or a points victory. Some settings are better for beginners—you can adjust the strength of your opponent and apply "underdog advantage," where you'll get help if you're losing. Others are just about personal taste. You can also change up your controls—we preferred using "B" for jump, for instance.

Choose your fighter

There are over 70 playable characters, and unlocking them all is part of the fun. There are characters from the big Nintendo games—*Mario*, *Pokémon*, *Zelda*, *Kirby*—but also from less well-known classics like *Star Fox*, *Mega Man*, *Kid Icarus*, and *Metroid*, and many from outside the world of Nintendo like *Sonic*, *Castlevania*, and *Final Fantasy*. Putting your character on random at first is a good idea, because it helps you learn which fighters you prefer.

Smashing backgrounds

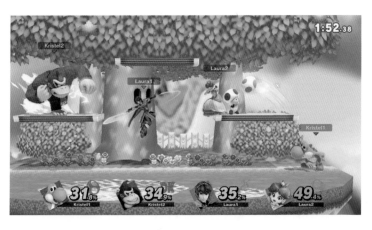

The real joy for many Nintendo nerds lies in the battlegrounds, where you can play in arenas based on current Nintendo games but also the retro worlds of *Duck Hunt* and *F-Zero*, a Game Boy screen playing *Kirby*, and even one of the LCD Game & Watch systems. But the basic battle areas are the easiest for new players.

Miitopia

Star rating: ⭐⭐⭐⭐⭐

The ability to make a Mii was a major feature of the Wii (that's where the name comes from), and though it's less of a thing on the Switch, *Miitopia* brings it right back. It's an interesting mix of RPG and social games —set in a fantasy world, you need to make friends among your fellow kingdom-dwellers, with the aim of winning their loyalty so you can lead them into battle and defeat the Dark Lord. This involves quite a lot of hanging out at the inn, and making sure everyone's fed.

Top Tip!

The horse is more valuable in battle than any Mii—make sure all your Miis have a good relationship with it!

Independent working

You don't control everything done by your army of Miis—you give them roles and equipment, but they make their own decisions. Some players might find this frustrating, but if you want a strategy game where you don't have to manage every little thing your troops do, this is the one for you.

Kirby Star Allies

The pink balloon dude is another classic character from the Nintendo stable, and his games are noted for their imaginative approach. In *Star Allies*, Kirby assembles an adventuring party by throwing hearts at enemies to turn them into friends—a cute idea that really affects your strategy. The main game is pretty easy—good for younger players—but there are extra challenges in the downloadable updates, and the Heroes in Another Dimension mode will keep you going for some time.

Top Tip!

You can use the Dream Palace between levels to change up your party—but remember, you can only do this once per stage!

Metroid Dread

Star rating:

Nintendo's *Metroid* series has been going since 1986 and created its own genre—games based on exploring and unlocking pieces of a large interconnected map are known as "Metroidvania". *Metroid Dread* is a slick update of the original's side-scrolling gameplay, mixing puzzle elements with combat and some nailbiting escapes from tight corners. Once again you play bounty hunter Samus Aran: this time she's been sent after a shape-shifting parasite on the planet ZDR. Parts of it are tricky, and it can be frustrating at first, but once you get to grips with everything Samus can do, it's really engrossing.

Terraria

Star rating: ⚪⚪⚪⚪⚪

The biggest challenger to *Minecraft*'s crown as the king of sandbox games, *Terraria* goes for a different visual style: it's a 2D side-scrolling game with a SNES-style graphics. Like *Minecraft*, though, it generates a new world for each new game, so each time is different—and you have to explore, build structures, and collect items. It doesn't have the same flexibility as *Minecraft*—so you won't be building vast cities in *Terraria* – but its combat and backstory are more fun.

Top Tip!
Keep your items until later in the game, rather than selling them early—wait until mega accessories and weapons are available!

Bossing around

The design of *Terraria*'s bosses is great and about as monstrous as you can get in this pixelated form—the Eye of Cthulhu and the Wall of Flesh are especially gruesome. And though you can tackle these bosses in your own time, summoning them when you're ready, they're pretty challenging! You need to be prepared for each fight, and two-player cooperation really helps.

Hollow Knight

Star rating:

This 2D adventure game sees you play as a nameless Knight, battling through the ruins of the kingdom of Hallownest. It looks incredible—every character is beautifully designed, and each level offers something new— even the backgrounds are fascinating. It's also cute—but don't be fooled, because *Hollow Knight* is absolutely rock hard. At first, you may feel like it's not worth it. But if you're patient, you'll be rewarded—the combat system seems straightforward, but takes time to master. Working out the best way to use the Charms you buy from NPCs is vital!

Top Tip!
Fight enemies in the air—you can be swifter there than on the ground.

Face your ghost

When you die in *Hollow Knight*, the money you've built up doesn't vanish—it's held by the ghost of your former self. If you want it back, you'll have to slay the ghost! You also need to do this to keep full capacity on your Soul Vessel, which is even more essential. Soul enables you to regenerate health, and you'll struggle to complete boss battles without it.

New arrivals

There's also the 30th anniversary Kirby game, *Kirby and the Forgotten Land*; the long-awaited sequel *Hollow Knight: Silksong*, which sees Hornet climb to the top of a shining citadel; and more paint-hurling action in *Splatoon 3*.

THE ULTIMATE SWITCH QUIZ

How much have you learned about the Switch? Test your knowledge here—and turn the page for the answers!

1. How do you take a screenshot on the Switch?

2. Which two retro consoles can you play via Switch Online?

3. What three games are included in Super Mario 3D All Stars?

4. What's the name of Luigi's ghost dog?

5. What is Cuphead's brother called?

6. Which party game inspired Among Us?

7. What kind of animal is BK in Donut County?

8. What country is the Galar region of Pokémon based on?

9.
Who scores your photos in New Pokémon Snap?

10.
Who's the villain of Ring Fit Adventure?

11.
What's the bestselling game of all time?

12.
What do you drop out of at the start of a Fortnite match?

13.
Who's the hero of Hades?

14.
What are the two arcade games in the Stardrop Saloon in Stardew Valley?

15.
What two things can you earn in Animal Crossing: New Horizons?

16.
What console was the original version of Link's Awakening made for?

17.
Who created Mario, Zelda, and Pikmin?

18.
What are the creatures in Unravel Two called?

19.
Which two Nintendo Switch games feature Mario and Sonic?

20.
In which game would you fight the Wall of Flesh?

Quiz answers

1. The square button on the left Joy-Con
2. The NES and the SNES
3. *Super Mario 64, Super Mario Sunshine and Super Mario Galaxy*
4. Polterpup
5. Mugman
6. Mafia
7. Raccoon
8. United Kingdom
9. Professor Mirror
10. Dragaux
11. *Minecraft*
12. The Battle Bus
13. Zagreus
14. *Journey of the Prairie King* and *Junimo Kart*
15. Bells and NookMiles
16. Game Boy
17. Shigeru Miyamoto
18. Yarnys
19. *Mario and Sonic at the Tokyo Olympic Games 2020* and *Super Smash Bros. Ultimate*
20. *Terraria*

Index

Among Us – 33
Animal Crossing: New Horizons – 52
Arms – 45
Carnival Games – 45
Cuphead – 32
Donut County – 35
Escapists, The – 34
FIFA – 47
Fitness Boxing 2: Rhythm and
    Exercise – 44
Fortnite – 48
Hades – 49
Hollow Knight – 75
Hyrule Warriors: Age of Calamity – 61
Just Dance – 44
Kirby Star Allies – 73
Legend of Zelda: Breath of the
    Wild – 58
Legend of Zelda: Link's
    Awakening – 57
Legend of Zelda: Skyward Sword
    HD – 60
Luigi's Mansion 3 – 26
Mario + Rabbids Kingdom Battle – 69
Mario and Sonic at the Olympic
    Games Tokyo 2020 – 24
Mario Golf: Super Rush – 18
Mario Kart 8 Deluxe – 20
Mario Party Superstars – 22
Mario Tennis Aces – 24
Metroid Dread – 73
Miitopia – 72
Minecraft – 46
Minecraft Dungeons – 46
Monster Hunter Rise – 49
New Pokémon Snap – 39
Night in the Woods – 32
Overcooked 2 – 51
Paper Mario: The Origami King – 25
Pikmin 3 Deluxe – 64

Plants vs. Zombies: Battle For
    Neighborville – 51
Pokémon Legends: Arceus – 38
Pokémon Sword & Shield – 37
Pokémon Unite – 39
Pokémon: Let's Go,
    Pikachu/Eevee! – 38
Rayman Legends – 67
Ring Fit Adventure – 42
Rocket League – 47
Sayonara Wild Hearts – 35
Sonic Mania – 66
Splatoon 2 – 68
Stardew Valley – 50
Super Bomberman R – 69
Super Mario 3D All-Stars – 19
Super Mario 3D World + Bowser's
    Fury – 23
Super Mario Maker 2 – 23
Super Mario Odyssey – 17
Super Mario Party – 22
Super Smash Bros. Ultimate – 70
Terraria – 74
Unravel Two – 65
Untitled Goose Game – 31

Ultimate Switch Checklist

- [ ] Unlocked Gold Mario in *Mario Kart 8 Deluxe*

- [ ] Completed either the fossil, insect, or fish collections in *Animal Crossing: New Horizons*

- [ ] Completed the Pokédex in *Pokémon Sword* or *Pokémon Shield*

- [ ] Unlocked all available fighters in *Super Smash Bros. Ultimate*

- [ ] Collected all seven Chaos Emeralds in *Sonic Mania*

- [ ] Completed all levels of *Untitled Goose Game* before the church bells ring

- [ ] Defeated the *Hollow Knight*

- [ ] Completed all the Shrines in *Breath of the Wild*

- [ ] Reached XP level 100 on any season of *Fortnite*

- [ ] Unlocked the Cowboy Hat in *Stardew Valley*

- [ ] Collected all the Teensies in *Rayman Legends*

- [ ] Defeated the Ender Dragon in *Minecraft*

- [ ] Defeated the Wall of Flesh in *Terraria*

- [ ] Defeated Dragaux in *Ring Fit Adventure*

- [ ] Defeated MegaDragonBowser in *Mario + Rabbids Kingdom Battle*

- [ ] Obtained the True Master Sword in *Skyward Sword HD*

- [ ] Collected over 500 Power Moons in *Super Mario Odyssey*